PRAISES FOR

KEEP IT 100

"When I read the dedication and saw: "to everyone who's heard Fatman Scoop say 'you got a $20 bill, put your hands up,' and couldn't put their hands up..." I knew this book would speak directly to my spirit.

Being an entrepreneur, you deal with constant pressure. I suffer from anxiety and self-doubt at times. I'm human. And reading this book during those low moments has been a revelation for me - inspiration in bite-sized nuggets that are relatable, encouraging and often times hilarious."

– Everette Taylor,
Jr - Entrepreneur

"This book took me back to 2015 when I was trying to get my head clear. It's simple yet profound principals like this that helped me break through and get to where I am today. Dope job with this Michell, I think this will help aspiring creatives especially. Has the right touch of humor too. LOL"

– Masego,
Musician

"As I sit on the bare floor of my new apartment with just an air mattress and a dream, I am grateful to read the words in Michell's book. God answers your prayers through people. Michell is a prayer answered for a friend of wisdom - a divine vulnerability that softly breaks through the surface with comedic blows. His words in this book are relatable, sweet but not sugar-coated truths that help us to make sense of the overwhelming plights of a young intellectual creative. Thank you for existing, being a voice, writing your Instagram captions & taking the challenge to be yourself in this world."

– Olivia Jade Khoury,
Writer

KEEP IT 100

Michell C. Clark

Daily affirmations for millennials who are tired of being called millennials.

13th & Joan books may be purchased for educational, business or sales promotional use. For information, please email the Sales Department at sales@13thandjoan.com

DEDICATION

To everyone who knows that growing up is a scam...

To everyone who battles fervently against Seasonal Ashiness Syndrome...

To everyone who passionately screams every word to Outkast's "Caroline" as often as possible...

To everyone who loves life's possibilities while fearing its uncertainties...

To everyone who's ever felt like their prayers went unheard...

To everyone who's heard Fatman Scoop say "you got a $20 bill, put your hands up," and couldn't put their hands up...

Thank you for existing. This book is for you.

"My childlike creativity, purity and honesty

Is honestly being crowded by these
grown thoughts.

Reality is catching up with me,

Taking my inner child - I'm fighting for custody."

– Kanye West

INTRODUCTION

My struggle was orchestrated by a higher power - I just didn't know it. I took longer to write this book than originally intended. Depression, anxiety, and lack of confidence hampered my creative process. I beat myself up for procrastinating, which only added to the waves of emotions in my mind.

All of these delays made time for Ardre Orie, the owner of a publishing house called 13th and Joan, to discover me on social media, take a liking to my Instagram captions, and ask me if I had any plans to write a book. My original plan was to self-publish and see what happened. Talk about silver lining. Talk about God's timing.

It's appropriate that I found my publisher on social media, as many of the quotes that make up the framework of this book were first published on my social media accounts. I took 100 short passages that I've written and wrote 100 words about each of them. This book is inspirational, sarcastic, vulnerable, honest, and authentic. I mean every single word. Thank you for reading.

ACKNOWLEDGEMENTS

Thank you to Ardre Orie for empowering me to transition from lifelong writer to first time author.

Thank you to Jacques Bastien for transforming my jumbled ideas into a book cover that could double as my mixtape cover.

Thank you to Duanecia Evans for reminding me that I'm good enough and that I know what I'm doing, when my palms are sweaty, knees weak, mom's spaghetti.

KEEP IT 100

{1}

EVERYONE WITH A LONG TERM PLACE IN YOUR LIFE NEEDS TO APPRECIATE YOUR IMPERFECTIONS.

I remember a particular point in my life where I was paralyzed by everyday decisions, such as what clothing to wear or what my twitter avatar should be. I wanted to be "good" or "cool" enough to fit the preferences of the people around me. Mad stressful. It was a huge weight, and no way for a young boss in the making to live. I stopped all that. There's a fine line between wanting to make a good impression and becoming a slave to the opinions of others. Y'all don't like me? Cool. I'm true to myself. Life is easier.

{2}

FOCUS ON THINGS WITHIN YOUR CONTROL.

I wish that Chick Fil A would be open every Sunday, and that I had never been forced to play clarinet in band during high school. Unfortunately, things like that are out of my control. I can't change them. I find solace by waiting until Monday to purchase multiple spicy chicken sandwiches, and taking charge of the things that I can control in the meantime. My habits, my thoughts, and my actions, for example. I can take action on a consistent basis and change my whole life. The obstacles will always be there, but they won't matter in the end.

{3}

IF YOU FAIL, OWN IT. COME BACK STRONGER THE NEXT DAY.

My wi-fi is too slow. My dog peed on my computer, so I can't type anymore. I could start that project, but I have plans to watch every single episode of Bob's Burgers instead. These statements all have some degree of truth to them. They're also cop-outs. Excuses. They're excellent for eliminating guilt, but terrible for facilitating the accomplishment of things that matter, such as making progress and leveling up. Sometimes, we resort to excuses. The most productive, successful people avoid leaning on them as often as possible. Don't be afraid to hold yourself accountable. You have barriers to break.

{4}

LONG TERM SUCCESS IS MORE IMPORTANT THAN SHORT TERM WINS. YOU NEED BALANCE TO MAINTAIN.

Don't believe the motivational memes. That "rise and grind" thing is a hoax. Constantly pressuring yourself to work without a break, from dawn until dusk, is not the best thing for the human psyche. It's also bad for your inner glo. The hardest workers, the ones who shun sleep and recovery time for what they think is "progress," aren't always the most successful. You need rest. You need time to reflect and consider alternate perspectives.The human brain functions most efficiently in relatively short rest/ work cycles. You are a human being. Take a break. Live a little. Stay woke.

{5}

OVERSLEEPING AND RUSHING TO WORK BUILDS CHARACTER.

Another work day morning has arrived. You still feel exhausted when your alarm clock goes off. You blink a few times. Suddenly, another hour has magically flown by and you're still in bed. You finally arrive at the office - flustered, tired, and without a cell phone charger. What can you even do at this point? You laugh. Laugh at yourself. Laugh at your coworker with the ashy elbows. Find a way to keep it moving, and recognize that the day is still young. There's plenty of time to turn the day back around, but that's up to you. Go prosper.

{6}

ALWAYS TREAT YOUR COSIGN LIKE IT MEANS SOMETHING.

The world can be overwhelming. Too much to accomplish. Too much to think about. Too much to absorb. We have to pick and choose what things to devote time and attention to. We use our best judgement. That being said, if you're constantly making recommendations that don't pan out in our favor, why should we listen to you? Whenever you cosign something, it should mean something. It shouldn't be a mindless gesture. Your cosign is a precious resource, but if overused it will become a meaningless formality that bears no weight - not even to you. Be selective. Protect your cosign.

{7}

BE THANKFUL FOR THE LIFE YOU HAVE, DESPITE ITS IMPERFECTIONS.

In a world full of first world problems and "what's your wi-fi network" conversation starters, it can be easy to forget how good life is. It's easy to forget that some of the opportunities we might take for granted could be seen as life changing for other people. Whatever your circumstances might be, it's important to take time to appreciate the positive things you have going on. Being generally thankful makes it easier to maintain a positive outlook. Don't be the grumpy cat of your friend circle, because we all know that cats are evil. Remain thankful no matter what.

{8}

REMEMBER YOUR BIG PICTURE GOALS. DON'T GET LOST IN THE DETAILS.

There's probably some perfect metaphor or anecdotal story about why you shouldn't get lost in the details. I'm sure it's there. However, if I continued to search my brain for that picture perfect introduction and stalled out in the process, that would probably go against the message I intend to convey. The message? Don't let perfectionist tendencies stop you from taking action. If you can plan ahead, but still go with the flow, you'll be able to keep moving despite whatever obstacles might arise. There's always room for improvement, but taking initiative to start something new is admirable in itself.

{9}

YOU HAVE MORE CONTROL OVER YOUR LIFE THAN YOU THINK.

You ever get tired of feeling like you know exactly how your day will go before it even starts? Sometimes a daily routine can start to feel like a trap. We get so comfortable with our habits that we let them steal our sense of adventure. Before you know it, you're falling asleep at work, and probably being made into a meme. Circumstances can be limiting, but we can't let them become definitive. Maybe you want to change your whole life. Maybe you just want to switch up a few small things. Either way, it's time to get started. Now.

{10}

TAKE TIME FOR YOURSELF WHEN YOU NEED IT.

There's always at least four things on your to-do list, five people you're supposed to call, and six e-mails you should have replied to before you started watching *Family Guy* last night. When was the last time you were awake, fully relaxed, disconnected from all forms of human interaction, and free of worry? Easier said than done, but forcing yourself to create the physical environment and mental space that facilitates such a level of self-care is restorative. We all need that degree of restoration in the midst of a life filled with so many jagged edges and unexpected plot twists.

{11}

TRUST GOD'S TIMING.

Do you know how many times I've wanted to put a crying Jordan face on a picture of White Jesus? Why would God allow me to go through some of the difficulties that I've faced? I ask this question often. Anger. Confusion. Disappointment. These emotions are prevalent during life's darkest moments. We don't have the capacity to understand why our lives turn out the way that they do. We don't need to. We don't have to understand why everything in life happens the way it does if we truly trust that God is working everything out for the greater good.

{12}

EVERY TIME YOU TAKE AN L, SOMETHING BETTER COMES BACK AROUND.

A lot of days, I feel like Bugs Bunny and Daffy Duck in Space Jam before Michael Jordan gave them the "secret stuff" - just getting punched in the face, over and over again. You know what, though? I'm still here. I'm still thriving. I've taken enough losses to understand that a loss isn't really a loss. It's a prompt to switch directions. Reassess. Reevaluate. You take the losses in stride, and allow lessons learned to mold you into a better version of yourself. That better version of yourself is more ready than ever to receive those blessings around the corner.

{13}

EVERY DAY WON'T BE EASY, BUT YOU STILL HAVE TO SHOW UP.

Something is going to go wrong, today. Even if your accident-prone coworker doesn't make something explode in the break room, and nobody's grandmother cuts you off driving 40 miles per hour in the fast lane. Just like yesterday, and the day before that, some sort of less than ideal situation will occur. It could be one huge thing. It could be a bunch of little things. There will never be a perfect day. You're still here, though. Take those less than ideal circumstances and push them aside. Focus on the things you can control, and you'll be golden. Major key.

{14}

DO IT WITHOUT PERMISSION, ON YOUR OWN CONDITIONS.

Chances are, nobody is going to walk up to you tomorrow and say, "hey, now would be a great time to make that big change you've been wanting to make." Honestly, I wouldn't mind if Morgan Freeman would narrate my entire life, and tell me exactly when to do that one big thing I've been planning. Unfortunately, I don't have the budget for that. You probably don't, either. You have to take it upon yourself to take action. Don't wait to be told. Don't wait for permission. Don't wait for an invitation. Push forward today, and watch your life change.

{15}

EVEN IF YOU LOSE EVERYTHING, YOU STILL HAVE WILLPOWER.

One time in college, I was so broke that I briefly considered dating a woman who worked at the chicken spot on campus just so I could get some free three piece meals. Not the proudest point of my life, but I made it through. Now I eat like an adult. We all make it through these situations. One thing you will always have? Willpower. It's the thing that will push you forward, no matter what. Never stop believing that you deserve better, and never stop feeling like you can work towards those long term achievements you know you deserve.

{16}

BEING UNAFRAID TO LOSE IS EMPOWERING.

You are going to take losses in life. They are inevitable. Bank on it. Even Michael Jordan played for the Wizards. The beautiful thing about life is that there are so many chances to learn from your losses, rebound, and win. In order to truly grow and learn, you can't afford to be afraid of the losses. You need to move like you know victories will come in due time. Walk with confidence, and remember that even if you don't succeed this time around, another opportunity will come. Channel your energy into putting your best foot forward. You'll surprise yourself.

{17}

EVERYTHING WORTH BUILDING TAKES TIME.

As much as I'd love to accomplish all of my essential life goals and be ridiculously wealthy by the middle of next week, that's not how the world is set up. Never forget that Diddy was a paperboy way before he was a billionaire. He had to earn it, just like you do. You wouldn't appreciate your proudest moments if you didn't have to work for them. Learning to appreciate the process is how we are able to continue to press forward. Don't be afraid to envision exactly where you're going to be when the work begins to pay off.

{18}

DON'T SELL YOURSELF SHORT.

Humility is important. Recognizing that you have a lot left to learn is admirable. It's indicative of someone who's still growing. You don't have to diminish your accomplishments in order to be humble. You don't have to discount the work you've done thus far to appease people who don't see value in your qualifications. Even if you're just starting a new career or creative endeavor, a proactive and diligent mentality is worth being proud of. Committing to actualizing your dreams is worth celebrating. The work is just beginning, but some people didn't make the choice to clock in. You did.

{19}

BE PATIENT WITH YOURSELF.

It's amazing to know that you can do whatever you want in this world. The key word? Can. It's possible. The problem? It's often frustrating when we don't get the results we want as quickly as we'd expect. We start to blame ourselves. We lose excitement. We settle. This isn't the way that things have to be, but it's a very easy path to travel. Mediocrity is very easy to achieve, but very rarely offers the sense of accomplishment that a more ambitious, purpose-driven journey will provide. Allow yourself time to develop and grow into the ultimate "you." Keep going.

{20}

YOU CAN'T CHANGE EVERY SITUATION. YOU CAN ALWAYS SEEK DEEPER UNDERSTANDING.

I daydream about how different life would be if I were born wealthy. What if I were the son of the owner of Popeyes and spent life surrounded by opulence, decadence, and greasy deliciousness? My daydreams permanently reside in a different dimension, so I'm left with what's real. What's real isn't always glamorous, but the fact that we're alive to experience it is a blessing. Time reveals that some of the worst situations we endure are part of a bigger plan that we don't understand in the heat of the moment. Allow yourself to reflect and benefit from that understanding.

{21}

IF YOU WANT IT TO BE A GREAT DAY, IT'S GONNA BE A GREAT DAY.

No matter how thoroughly I plan for tomorrow, I still don't know what will happen. I know which three songs I'll hear on the radio all day, but that's it. What matters is that I understand that my lack of ability to predict the details of my day doesn't correlate with a lack of ability to determine my direction over time. The speed bumps will come. So will the opportunities. Remain level headed as the cycle continues to repeat itself. Interpret every day you spend on this Earth as a blessing, and it becomes easier to roll with the punches.

{22}

THE LESS YOU FLEX, THE EASIER THINGS FLOW.

Before Rae Sremmurd made it clear once and for all, the truth was still easy to find. You don't have to flex. It's better if you don't. It's one thing to be genuinely happy about your success and progression as an individual. It's another thing entirely to run around rubbing the aforementioned successes in other people's faces like you're one of those ladies with free perfume samples at a mall kiosk. You don't have to flaunt your achievements in order to be appreciated. You'll find that more people are genuinely happy for you if you accept your wins with grace.

{23}

STILL NO HATERATION OR HOLLERATION IN THIS DANCERIE.

Life is short. I don't have time to expend energy actively hating anybody, for any reason. I'm too busy trying to win at life, pay my rent, and figure out which one of Beyoncé's cousins might be single. I'd rather be totally indifferent to the life of someone that I don't rock with than to spend my valuable time devoting negative thought to them. That will allow me to save more time for world domination schemes. You're never going to click with everyone; in the end, it's better to just live and let live than to actively oppose other people.

{24}

TAKE A BREAK WHEN YOU NEED TO.

A big part of our culture is obsessed with achievements, status, wealth, and progression. We're overexposed to news in regards to the incredibly wealthy and famous, to the point that it can make us feel inadequate if we're not careful to keep things in perspective. Many of us seek to constantly be productive, but what we forget is that it's important to feel peace and happiness in the present. There will always be improvements to be made. Find time to kick back and relax a bit, even if your to-do list is out of control and your hairline ain't crispy.

{25}

BE BRAVE. PUSH YOURSELF.

You know that thing you've been putting off for three months that you think will really take you to the next level? Are you putting it off because you're busy, or are you avoiding it for a different reason? Are you afraid? We tend to avoid things that we're unfamiliar with, because of the fear that we'll fail, or look foolish. Put your all into the things that you're passionate about, and don't be afraid to fail in the process. You can try, fail, try again, and succeed. Or, you could sit around forever wondering "what would have happened if..."

{26}

JUST BECAUSE YOU'RE IMPERFECT DOESN'T MEAN YOU'RE UNDESERVING.

I deserve to be happy on days when I come up short. I deserve to be happy when my barber's on vacation, I go to the guy in the first chair ,and he gives my hairline a little bit of a Young Dro "Shoulder Lean" to the left. We deserve to be happy in the moment despite less than opportune circumstances. We deserve to be happy in the midst of failure and uncertainty. We deserve to be happy, even if we haven't done everything we've set out to accomplish. Don't let any situations dictate the way you feel about yourself.

{27}

NOBODY'S GOT IT ALL TOGETHER. EVERYBODY'S DEALING WITH SOMETHING BENEATH THE SURFACE.

We're all imperfect humans. The people we call "great" are struggling with issues just like the rest of us. They become "great" because they succeed in spite of it all. We all have to confront uncomfortable truths, deal with paralyzing vulnerabilities, and accept the consequences of failure. We all have things that we're not proud of. Things that don't represent what we're truly capable of. Even Jay-Z had a *Kingdom Come* moment. When you interact with people, consider that they may be more broken, hurt, or afraid than they'd like to admit. We're all living complex lives below the surface.

{28}

LET'S ALL JUST ORDER PIZZA AND START OVER AGAIN TOMORROW.

Comeback stories are the best stories, but it's hard to enjoy being the underdog in real life before the tide starts to turn. Life isn't a television sitcom with perfectly timed jokes to distract from the tough times. It can be difficult to find the silver lining after making it through the worst days. Sometimes, you just need to take three deep breaths, order a pizza with all the fixings, and remind yourself that a lot can change in 24 hours. Don't allow yesterday's struggles to cloud your thoughts to the point that they prevent you from seeing today's opportunities.

{29}

DAILY REMINDER: THIS WORK ISN'T GONNA DO ITSELF.

You can research and plan for as long as you want to. Go to all of the networking mixers, have all the surface level conversations, and post all of the "rise and grind" pictures on social media, to your heart's content. Working smart and planning ahead are both important, but nothing will replace the value of actually rolling up your sleeves and getting to work. Starting new ventures may be frightening, but you have to actually take those risks so that you can learn how to get better and see the results that you want, in due time. Get started.

{30}

BREAK OUT OF EVERY BOX THAT THEY ATTEMPT TO PUT YOU IN.

People who defy expectations often seem brilliant and innovative after they've accomplished the goals they've set out to achieve. A lot of these people don't become visible to us until they've begun to achieve those goals. Those en route to being considered innovative and impactful are generally off putting or disorienting to a number of people, because they're disturbing the natural order that many people prefer. We like to be comfortable, but that's not what will create change. Unapologetically break out of the boxes that people intend to keep you inside of, if they're stopping you from fulfilling your purpose.

{31}

A LOT OF THINGS CAN CHANGE IN A MONTH OR TWO. DON'T LET THE PRESENT DICTATE YOUR OUTLOOK.

I hate to break it to you, but it's very improbable that the "special" person who's been leaving all your texts on "read at 8:15AM" will reply back. Fortunately, a lot of the other things you've been waiting on aren't bound to such predictable outcomes. Progress comes slowly some days, and quicker than we could ever imagine on at other times. It's important to continue finding ways to remain consistent with our efforts. There are times to be innovative with your approach. There are times to have faith in the process and let things change course in due time.

{32}

BE INTENTIONAL ABOUT SETTING TIME ASIDE FOR THINGS THAT MATTER.

Being busy is overrated. We see self-proclaimed hustlers bragging about being "too busy" every day, and patting themselves on the back for working hard from dawn to dusk. A strong sense of work ethic is commendable, but it's important to ask yourself one question: are you staying busy for the right reasons? It's easy to delude yourself into thinking that working as hard as possible for as long as possible will help you make progress. Be sure that the hard work you're putting in allows you to build a lifestyle full of the things that matter to you the most.

{33}

DISTRACTIONS ARE EVERYWHERE. DON'T LOSE SIGHT OF WHAT YOU'RE WORKING TOWARDS.

"Every opportunity that comes my way isn't meant for me." Besides being a great way to politely and philosophically decline pyramid scheme invitations from old "friends" who contact you on Facebook chat, this is a relevant phrase for life. We can't jump at every opportunity that comes our way. The world is complex, and always changing. People come and go. Temporary people can introduce long lasting concept and ideas into your life. You have to have the vision to understand which things you need to keep. Take the time to imagine your dream life, then build it piece by piece.

{34}

YOU MIGHT HAVE A MILLION DOLLAR IDEA ON GOOGLE DRIVE RIGHT NOW.

You could have the greatest idea in the world, but unless you have enough self belief and discipline to execute it, that idea means nothing. The difference between the average person and the trailblazer is that the latter refuses to accept that their current life path is something they are irrevocably tied to. Do you have it in you to be as tenaciously dedicated and focused as your favorite game changer was before they got all of their accolades? Your habits have to change before your life does. If you're waiting for that perfect time to get started, it's here.

{35}

A DIAMOND IN THE ROUGH IS STILL A DIAMOND.

Even when it has yet to reach its picture perfect, sparkling form, a diamond is still a diamond. Even though you're working on fully applying yourself in the best way possible, you are powerful. You're endowed with a unique combination of talent, circumstance, and experience that gives you the ability to make a distinct, positive impact in a way that no one else can. You're not there yet, wherever "there" is, and that's completely fine. Your glo up is on the way. Remind yourself that you are blessed beyond measure, and allow yourself the time to grow into those blessings.

{36}

SWEATPANTS ARE SACRED.

I'm not sure how I would be able to properly function in life without a few comfortable pairs of sweatpants to lounge around in when I just want to be alone and sing every word to Outkast's "Ms. Jackson" in my bathroom mirror. We all need those times. We need times to escape. You deserve to have moments where you're completely left to your own devices, with plenty of space to breathe. Take whatever things make you feel comfortable enough to sing Outkast in your bathroom mirror, and save them for those refreshing, restorative moments. Sweatpants are sacred. Get comfy.

{37}

DON'T COMPARE YOUR SCRIMMAGES TO OTHER PEOPLE'S HIGHLIGHT REELS.

It's easy to feel inadequate if you don't guard your thoughts. Scroll through social media and you'll see the things people want you to see. Ask someone how they're doing, and they're more likely to say "fine" than tell you how they really feel. We learn to keep our weak, vulnerable moments close to our chests. We rarely get the full, unbiased story of someone's journey. The people we view as role models, heroes, and celebrities are or have gone through just as much uncertainty and doubt as the rest of us. We all go through it. You're not alone.

{38}

YOU AIN'T GOTTA SHOOT EVERY SHOT.

"You never know until you try." That may be true, but you don't always have to find out firsthand whether something is meant for you or not. Trust your instincts. Trust what you've learned about yourself up to this point, and make sure that you set yourself up for shots you want to take. Shooters shoot, but snipers make the kill. It might not feel natural to remain motionless, waiting for the right target to fall in your sights. Force yourself to wait until the time is right, keep your eyes locked on the target, and take your BEST shot.

{39}

DON'T WAIT UNTIL YOU'RE UNCOMFORTABLE TO PUSH THE ENVELOPE.

Sprinting across campus to turn a term paper in at the last second was a college thrill. The allure of the rush is gone, though. As an adult I realize that I have to focus on putting forth my best effort, not just beating the clock. I can't afford to make everything a last minute rush. The results of my efforts extend beyond a semester. I'm not the only one who struggles with procrastination. We have to own that. Not tomorrow, but now. It's exciting to hit buzzer beaters, but why wait until the fourth quarter to seal the deal?

{40}

GOD DON'T EVER GIVE ME NOTHIN' I CAN'T HANDLE.

Why, God? Why me? I've asked myself this question many times, using different words, and inspired by different occurrences. I asked "why" when Chipotle was out of steak. I asked "why" when the Washington Wizards drafted Kwame Brown. I asked "why" when I endured the most devastating failures of my life. Despite the traumatizing moments that you've endured, you can say one thing for certain. You're still here. Every struggle has given you new perspective, and provided you with tools to overcome future obstacles. Allow yourself to appreciate the struggle, even when you're still working your way out of it.

{41}

TODAY'S HABITS BUILD TOMORROW'S VICTORIES.

What are you doing with your time? Ask yourself this question. Ask it often. You're not in control of everything in your life, and there will always be plot twists, but you always have choices to make. Those choices you make today can add up to create a future that you can't even imagine yet. Remind yourself that the habits you form and maintain will propel you towards maximizing your potential, your fulfillment and your legacy. Choose to be exceptional. It's far from easy, but it's not meant to be easy. By definition, everyone can't be great. You can, though.

{42}

ENERGY SPENT WORRYING IS ENERGY WASTED.

The world is way too complex for any of us to predict. Just ask your local meteorologist. Somebody with a lot more wisdom and a much better credit score than I once said that worrying is the interest you pay on a debt you may not owe. I'm no economist, but I definitely agree with this sentiment. Why waste energy that could be spent crying over Drake lyrics on something that MIGHT happen? It's a losing equation. Prepare for the possibilities, but understand that no amount of worrying will ever actually benefit you. Put your energy into more positive things.

{43}

DON'T BE AFRAID TO UNEQUIVOCALLY TELL SOMEONE, "NAH."

It's amazing how comfortable certain acquaintances in my life can be with asking me for unprecedented favors. It's equally amazing at how comfortable I am with saying "nah, bruh, I can't buy 10 copies of your mixtape." It's not mean; It's not selfishness. It's a necessity. I'm a human being with basic needs. If I'm struggling to take care of myself, there's no way I can consistently, substantially help someone else. If you're uncomfortable telling someone "no" when it's necessary, you could very well find your own well being and happiness at risk. Don't get caught up in the hype.

{44}

YOU HAVE HELLA THINGS TO DO TODAY. YOU'RE GONNA GET HELLA THINGS DONE TODAY.

I gotta confess - if I don't pick a song for my alarm clock that's forceful enough to jolt me out of dreaming about bacon cheeseburgers and waffle fries, I'll definitely press the snooze button at least ten times every day. I know myself. Sometimes, part of the reason I'm so slow to get up is a degree of worry about exactly how busy my day is about to be. Oftentimes, we find ourselves with a seemingly impossible amount of tasks to accomplish one day. Thinking about things one step at a time can help with the feeling of being overwhelmed.

{45}

TODAY'S STRUGGLES EQUIP YOU FOR TOMORROW'S BREAKTHROUGH.

Being broke is trash. That being said, it made me an expert at making tasty, somewhat healthy "struggle meals" during my college years. They probably weren't actually healthy at all, but that's besides the point. I didn't care about that in college, I was just busy wishing I had enough money for a large pizza and a bottle of Hennessy. That being said, I can appreciate that those struggle years taught me how to be a billion times more resourceful and creative in the kitchen. There's always a silver lining, no matter how long it takes you to find it.

{46}

LIFE BE LIFEING.

After spending enough time on this Earth, I've come to the conclusion that God has to be a comedian. He's definitely watched The Chappelle Show at least a few times. There's no way the plot twists in my life could be this ironic without some sort of divine intervention. Life just has a way of continuing to find ways to keep things interesting. I can never truly predict what will happen next, but I can teach myself to be thankful and roll with the punches, regardless. Life is going to keep throwing surprises your way, so just enjoy the ride.

{47}

DON'T LET UNFAMILIARITY DETER YOU FROM CONTINUING TO GROW.

You can't afford to shy away from situations that make you nervous if those situations will help you in the long run. It's not easy to confront the unfamiliar, especially when consequences are uncertain. That being said, nervousness can be a good thing, depending on perspective. It's a sign that you're stepping out of your comfort zone, which is the only way you'll truly learn and grow as a person. Time is short; we only have so many days on this planet. If you're committed to being the best "you" that you can be, don't shy away from new challenges.

{48}

LET MY PEOPLE GLO.

Sometimes we're afraid of the success of others. We're scared to praise the accomplishments of other people, due to the fear that their glo will block or diminish our own shine. This is a defensive instinct that stops us from reaping the benefits of communal celebration and collaboration. Sharing in the joy of others' successes is absolutely one of the best things you can do to ignite your own hustle. You're endowed with a unique set of experiences, characteristics, influences, and circumstances that equip you to impact the world in a way that nobody else can. We can all eat.

{49}

IF YOU'VE NEVER BEEN CURVED IN YOUR LIFE, YOU'RE NOT AIMING HIGH ENOUGH.

There's an inherent thrill that comes with taking risks, but there's also a cumulative reward that comes with being willing to continuously put yourself out there over time. You don't take risks because you know success is guaranteed. You take risks because you want success more than you want comfort, and you know that if you don't win this time, you'll be back ready to win next week. It's impossible to test and redefine your limits if you never scratch the ceiling you've been told is in place. Find the impossible things you're excited to accomplish, and get after them.

{50}

OPTIMISM IS EASY WHEN LIFE IS GREAT. OPTIMISM IS EMPOWERING WHEN LIFE HITS YOU IN THE CHEST.

When things don't go my way for an extended period of time, my instinct is to either eat a ridiculous amount of potato chips, or to search for the nearest couch to take a nap on. Sleep and snacks are both undeniably important, but the most important thing that's gonna help me turn things around during those moments is my mentality. You have to resist the urge to get down on yourself or upset with circumstances for extended periods of time. Rest if you need to, but never lose sight of how much power you have to change your situation.

{51}

DON'T SLEEP ON YOURSELF.

There is a huge, fundamental difference between what you have yet to accomplish and what you are unable to accomplish. For example, Donald Trump has the ability to not tweet like a middle school bully. We can't get caught up in our present day shortcomings to the point that we shame ourselves into a feeling of paralysis. Don't interpret people who are more accomplished than you as being "better" than you. More accomplished, more focused, more experienced? Potentially. That can change over time. You have plenty of growing to do, and falling in love with that process will yield dividends.

{52}

TRYING TO PLEASE EVERYONE IS A TRAP.

Treating people right is important, but sometimes the line between treating everyone right and trying to please everyone can get blurrier than JR Smith's court vision. The world is a better place when we're all kind to each other. No doubt. That being said, it's very difficult to give your goals and your self preservation the energy and attention that they require when you're too busy trying to keep everyone happy. What's the best way to truly add net value to the world? Become the best version of yourself, and help those who you can while in pursuit of that.

{53}

DEAD THE DISTRACTIONS.

This world is not conducive to the kind of intense, consistent focus required to construct exceptional things. In order to maximize yourself, that's just the kind of focus that you need. Whether you actively seek distractions or not, they are almost inevitably bound to spring up around you. Expect them. We're more connected with each other than ever before, and we're consequentially more easily pulled away from the things that matter the most. Keep your goals at the forefront of your mind, and don't allow your goals to become less ambitious because you're not committed to making time for them.

{54}

THERE'S NO SHORTCUT OR CHEAT CODE THAT CAN REPLACE CONSISTENCY.

If there were cheat codes to life, I would have already found the answers on Wikipedia or Sparknotes. I would be too busy traveling the world in search of exotic pizzas and Beyonce's single cousins to write this book. There are no cheat codes. Are people born into situations that give them advantages I would love to have? Yes. That being said, there's no shortcut for my next level up. We can definitely change our lives, but we have to chart our own courses and put in the work to make that happen. It's on us. Let's make it happen.

{55}

EVERYBODY GETS NERVOUS. THE CHAMPIONS PUSH THROUGH IT.

Being nervous isn't a fun feeling. There's no way around it. You know. Palms sweaty, knees weak, Mom's spaghetti and all that. That being said, if you're pushing yourself to become a better person, it's likely that you'll experience some temporary discomfort. Fear of some sort of failure is oftentimes at the center of nervousness. Feeling inadequate in the face of whatever situation may await you. Avoiding uncomfortable situations because of uncertain outcomes is a fantastic way to stay well within the confines of your comfort zone and your perceived limitations. That's not what you're here for, though. Is it?

{56}

CREATING SOMETHING OUT OF NOTHING MAKES THE REWARD SO MUCH SWEETER.

Building something long lasting from scratch is incredibly difficult, but once you make it happen no one can ever take that away from you. Don't romanticize being a self starter as being on some sort of magical journey where the path is clearly laid out for you. It'll be more difficult than you expect, and it will require exceptional levels of focus, discipline, and consistency. The painstaking process of succeeding against the odds will make the fruits of your labor that much sweeter. If this is truly what you want, don't let up until you get what you came for.

{57}

DON'T LET ANYONE ELSE DEFINE YOUR GOALS FOR YOU.

It's cool to respect someone's opinion. There's nothing wrong with valuing expertise, experience, or perspective. That being said, no one else has seen your entire life unfold the way that you have, and no one else has to live with the choices that you make as you chart your own course. Don't let anyone else have the final say in how you live your life. A lot of people want to live vicariously through others, but we can't forget that we still have our own lives to live. You deserve to achieve extraordinary success on your own terms. Believe that.

{58}

DON'T LOOK DOWN WHILE YOU CLIMB.

Rising above the standards you've set for yourself can be a disorienting experience because you have to alter your everyday life. You have to remove the things that make you feel secure and safe, because it's time to forge into the unknown. You're forcing yourself to change for the better. It's not a gentle or natural process. A lot of the people, habits, and expectations that had a degree of influence in your life have to be removed from the equation. You should feel thrown off. There's no convenient time to start this process. Start now, and don't look back.

{59}

DON'T LOSE YOURSELF IN PURSUIT OF THE COOL.

It's natural to desire a degree of acceptance from your peers. It's natural to seek out "the cool." We're not without need. We're not made to move through this world alone, devoid of encouragement and moral support. That being said, seeking acceptance can lead to losing track of what you stand for if you don't hold firmly to your foundations, your morals, and your dreams. If "the cool" is the only thing you seek, it's the only thing you can expect to hold on to. Lupe Fiasco taught us about the pitfalls of chasing "the cool". The point still stands.

{60}

SPEND LESS TIME BEING MAD AT UNFORTUNATE CIRCUMSTANCES AND MORE TIME LEARNING FROM THEM.

Some days are great. Some days are trash. That's life. Punching a hole in the wall won't change the fact that your sports team is garbage. Cussing somebody out might feel fantastic in the short term, but it (probably) won't make your life better. Life can be unpredictable, but it always provides plenty of lessons, if you're willing to listen. Those lessons don't come from the easy days, or from the victories you didn't have to fight for. If you're open and observant, you'll use unfortunate circumstances to pick up knowledge that will help you be successful in the future.

{61}

NEVER STOP BELIEVING THAT YOU CAN IMPROVE YOURSELF AND IMPROVE YOUR LIFE.

Have you ever hit rock bottom? Have you felt like you were stuck in a bad place, with no way out? Chances are, we've all been broken at some point in our lives. Life throws more things at us than we think we can handle. For as long as you live, you must not give up the belief that you can rebound from those rock bottom moments. You are imperfect, but you're resilient. You might have been broken, but you are not finished. Continue to remind yourself that you can make things better, no matter what life throws your way.

{62}

LEFTOVER PIZZA IS A GIFT FROM GOD.

You have to appreciate little things in life. When I was rich in my mind and broke in reality during my college years, leftover pizza was the best thing I had in life. If I woke up hangover free, and no one had eaten the pizza I had managed to purchase the night before? My life felt perfect. To this day, I'm still thankful when I wake up to leftover pizza in my fridge, even though my roommates have their own food now. Never lose your sense of appreciation for those little things, even if you know they'll be there.

{63}

DON'T MAKE THE MISTAKE OF WAITING FOR SOMEONE TO GIVE YOU WHAT YOU DESERVE.

Hard work is absolutely essential to achieving exceptional goals. That being said, don't make the mistake of believing that hard work is all that you need. You need to constantly search for the right opportunities, and actively put yourself into the positions that you need to be in. I don't believe in gatekeepers. They never came through for me. I don't believe that someone else will come along and magically put me in a position to accomplish my dreams. I believe in charting my own course, advocating myself, and putting myself on. Don't leave things up to fate. Take control.

{64}

THE WORK IS ALWAYS MORE IMPORTANT THAN THE TITLES.

We don't care if you have booking info in your twitter bio. We don't care what your business card says. We don't care what your LinkedIn profile says. What have you done in real life that can bring value to the world? What impact are you going to have on the world? I know that incompetence seems to be highly valued if you look at recent election results, but don't be fooled. The things you're actually prepared to bring to the table are way more important than the things you say you want to do. Take action. Titles are earned.

{65}

WHEN YOU REALLY WANT SOMETHING, THE EXCUSES DON'T MATTER ANYMORE.

It never mattered how hungover or sleepy I was. When I was growing up, I absolutely had to be at church every single Sunday. I really didn't want to get grounded, yelled at, or lectured about my life priorities, so I made sure to be on time to service at 11AM. Mostly. The excuses didn't matter. That's life. Even if you don't have parents, a boss, or someone else to hold you accountable, you have to prioritize the things you're truly committed to bringing to fruition in your life. Excuses are easy, but results are what the world will remember.

{66}

NEVER LET OUTSIDE OPINIONS DEFINE YOU.

Whether you're getting roasted on twitter, told you're not good enough at work, or slandered for mistakes that you've made in the past, outside opinions can have detrimental effects on the way that you see yourself. The key word is "can," because the rest is up to your interpretation. People will always have things to say, but remember that everyone's speaking from their own individual perspectives. Remember that the way you view yourself is what will determine how you carry yourself, how you behave yourself, and how you set yourself up for success in the future. Define yourself for yourself.

{67}

CREATION > COMPETITION

Competition is about constantly trying to be better than other people. It's reactive and unoriginal. Creation is about constructing something uniquely valuable that no one can take away from you. The former is a constant back and forth battle that you can't control. The latter is a process that takes patience and persistence, but can yield extraordinary results. When you're truly embracing the process of being the best version of yourself, you're not even worried about what the other person is building. When focusing on creation, you find yourself building things that no one else has been able to imagine.

{68}

NEVER LET PLAN B DISTRACT FROM PLAN A.

Safety nets become overrated when they evolve from a "just in case" option to an excuse to fall back on. It's good to plan for the worst, but not to the point that it allows you to stop pushing yourself to achieve the things that you really want. Don't get it twisted. I'm not telling you to quit your day job and wholeheartedly pursue your fantasy of being an international arm wrestling champion. What I am suggesting is that it's a much more fulfilling journey to pursue your dreams with discipline, confidence and aggression than to live a life unfulfilled.

{69}

FUEL YOUR FANTASIES.

Every single, amazing, accomplishment started off as a dream in someone's head, without any real life manifestation. Pioneers aren't given a clear road map with all of the keys to success. If you have exceptional goals, they'll seem strange, difficult, or inconceivable to most people. Most people don't have the mentality necessary to achieve extraordinary results. That doesn't mean you can't achieve them; it just means you have to remain steadfast You have to believe in yourself and your ability to accomplish your goals, just like the Toon Squad believed in Michael Jordan's ability to help them defeat the Monstars.

{70}

LIFE IS A TEST.

We are remarkably small, in the grand scheme of things. We use religion, morality, law, and science to attempt to bring order to the way we interpret the world. Humanity disagrees about each of these methods of interpretation. What you believe is your choice. I'll simply suggest this. Hold fast to the train of thought that will best equip you to become the best version of yourself. Choose to believe that life is simply a test, designed to push you to the limit as you pursue the excellence that you're capable of. Choose to embrace the challenges. Choose to win.

{71}

BIG OPPORTUNITIES DON'T COME WHEN YOU EXPECT THEM. YOU STILL HAVE TO BE READY.

Unless your crossover, cornrows, and interview quotes are as tight as Allen Iverson's, you can't skip practice. Hint: you can't skip practice. You will perform better when big opportunities come your way if you've been preparing all along, every day, to the best of your ability. If you're not getting ready to win, someone else is. If you're not working hard enough to prepare, someone else will likely be the better candidate for what you want. They might just take what could have been yours. Don't let a weak work ethic stop you from taking what's meant for you, homie.

{72}

BE HONEST WITH YOURSELF ABOUT WHAT'S HOLDING YOU BACK.

"It wasn't my time." "It wasn't meant to be." Sometimes, these phrases hold a degree of truth to them. Sometimes, these phrases are placeholders for people who are hesitant to admit their shortcomings. We are all imperfect. It might seem easier to shift blame onto things outside of our control. The problem is, mentally shifting blame elsewhere and avoiding self-assessment and self-accountability is an easy way to stay stuck. Do not beat yourself up for being imperfect, but do not grow comfortable in the belief that there's nothing more you can do to put yourself in a position to win.

{73}

MAKING A MISTAKE IS BETTER THAN INACTION.

I'm an internationally acclaimed, world class over thinker. I once spent an hour staring at a wall wondering whether or not crabs at the bottom of the ocean think that fish are flying. You can thank twitter for that one. At times I think too much about how to best achieve my goals. I plan ahead for ages, and forget to actually take action. We actually learn the most when we make mistakes. Mistakes aren't always fun to make, but they teach us what will not work, empowering us to move on find out what will. Make more mistakes, please.

{74}

STAYING AHEAD OF THE CURVE REQUIRES TAKING RISKS.

People laugh at you when you're figuring things out, and claim they supported you all along once you win. That's the way it goes when you're in the process of breaking the mold. To be a visionary requires a degree of vision others lack. You must be confident enough in your dream to push yourself to fulfill it, even when people laugh at you. Even when you haven't figured out every step you gotta take to get there. Take those risks, learn as you go along, and focus on the end state goals in lieu of the present day discomfort.

{75}

FIND SOMETHING WORTH REBELLING FOR.

Doing things that have already been done for people who've already seen them is a surefire way to be forgettable in the grand scheme of things. You weren't placed on this earth and subsequently given your unique set of abilities, experiences, and perspectives to be completely predictable and acceptable to the world for your entire life. Find something worth rebelling for. You don't have to stage a coup or burn down a small village, but finding a way to redefine a part of your life that doesn't spark something inside of you in its present state is an amazing rebirth.

{76}

NEVER EVER LOSE TRACK OF YOUR "WHY."

Have you ever felt lost in life? I have. Many times. I got to the point where I was considering giving pyramid schemes a try. I thought about calling back that Nigerian prince who kept leaving voicemails about inheritance money he wanted to give me. I felt lost. Not because of imperfect circumstances, but because of the way I was thinking about my life. I let other factors cloud my vision to the point that I was drifting, instead of moving forward. We can't afford to forget where we want to go when we're working so hard to get there.

{77}

YOU HAVE TO STUDY THE GAME BEFORE YOU CAN PUSH IT FORWARD.

I still have so much to learn. It doesn't matter how much I've done, or what I have planned in the present. Why? Because I need to absorb enough information and draw enough inspiration to be able to accomplish the things that I couldn't imagine two years ago, or six months ago, or last week. I believe that I'm meant to have an impact on this world that stretches beyond myself. We can never afford to feel like we've learned everything there is to learn if we truly want to be able to change the world from its present state.

{78}

AVOID THE PETTY AT ALL COSTS.

Being petty can be extremely satisfying, in the moment. I know. I mean, that's what I've been told by a distant acquaintance. I can't relate, because everyone knows that I'm a kind hearted, innocent soul every day of the week. Don't question this. That being said, I think we can all agree that there are times when we'd rather allow the petty to grow inside of us instead of pushing it away. The problem is, it's not going to help. You'll be happier in the long run if you channel your energy into the things that will ensure your success.

{79}

YOU CAN'T DEFEAT SOMEBODY WHO'S WALKING WITHIN THEIR PURPOSE.

Purpose is powerful. It allows you to push forward when others can't. It allows you to feel empowered when others choose the path of least resistance. A strong sense of purpose serves as insulation when the climate changes. If you're not careful, it's easy to get caught up in simply focusing on survival. It's understandable, but spending too much time operating in "survival mode" separates you from everything that makes you unique. Choose to explore your interests, and discover your passions. Choose to use your talents for the greater good. Choose to walk in your purpose. Choose to be undefeatable.

{80}

DON'T LET IMAGINARY BARRIERS IMPEDE YOUR GROWTH.

Internal barriers, or limitations that you place upon yourself, can change the way that you behave, if you let them. They can lead you to build habits that limit what you can accomplish in this world. If you're giving in to self-imposed limitations, people will treat you like those limitations are real. You have to separate true obstacles from things you're choosing to hide behind. Choose to cast aside any beliefs that you might have about what you can do. Set out to defy everyone's expectations about what you can accomplish - even your own. You're more powerful than you think.

{81}

IN IT. OF IT. STILL GREAT.

Many will preach the need to separate themselves from the ways of the world in order to maximize their potential. There's some validity to that. Focus is important. However, to decide that we are better than others is a slippery slope. I'm not better than anyone else. I'm not more exceptional. Some of us will choose to outwork others, some of us will get more opportunities, and some of us will just be downright lucky. When we begin to believe that we're "better" than other humans, dangerous things can start to happen. You might work harder, but you're not better.

{82}

MAKE YOUR OWN WAVE.

There's a time to fit into the pre-established order of the world, and there's a time to flip the table over, disrupt the scene, and create something entirely new. Successfully defying conventional wisdom requires exceptional knowledge of your surroundings and yourself, unshakeable focus, and a degree of confidence that many will temporarily view as foolishness. The people who make biggest impact and attain the biggest wins are those who solve a persisting problem within the world by altering the way society functions. It takes a lot of energy to create the wave, but once you do, the ride is amazing.

{83}

TAKE THE TIME TO FULLY EXECUTE YOUR IDEAS TO THE BEST OF YOUR ABILITY.

Some people choose to talk frivolously about the failures and successes of others, critiquing their mistakes and saying what they should have done differently. Other people choose to do the heavy lifting and struggling themselves, as they work towards accomplishing great achievements on their own terms. The former might temporarily capture the imagination and allow a degree of self-aggrandizement, while the latter is an arduous but inherently rewarding process that facilitates self actualization. Your life is too short and finite to choose anything but the latter. Commit to creating something that will change your life and the world. Commit wholeheartedly.

{84}

BE YOURSELF, AND THE THINGS THAT ARE MEANT FOR YOU WILL COME.

"Be you, that's when it sounds "be-au-tiful" was definitely a cringe-worthy line, but J. Cole-isms aside, it actually touches upon an extremely important concept. One of the best things any of us can do in this cole world is to recognize the value that we bring to the table when we're able to cast all our facades, fronts, and insecurities to the side. The "come up" will work out for you when you can't get enough of yourself. Allow yourself the liberation that comes from living in your truth, no matter what other people may think of it. Love yours.

{85}

PUT YOURSELF ON.

Life is unpredictable. Your final destination in this world is currently undetermined. It's possible to gauge where you might end up, but to base your future around your present situation is choosing to cast imagination to the side. It's disenchanting and limiting. The odds might be stacked against you, but that can change through your planning and efforts. You'll appreciate your progression so much more when you create something from nothing. If Audio Push can go from "Teach Me How To Jerk" to Shine," anything is possible. Make positive progress today. Take charge. Let nothing deter you. Put yourself on.

{86}

DON'T BE LOYAL TO ANYTHING OR ANYBODY THAT'S HARMFUL TO YOU.

Loyalty is an important and valuable virtue, but don't hold tight to it to the point that others can weaponize it against you. People, situations, and life in general can change quickly. Change can occur drastically and instantly, and it can also occur subtly over more extended periods of time. Be vigilant in regards to what you allow into your life, and what you allow to stay in your life. Check yourself consistently to ensure that you're not allowing yourself to be taken advantage of. You deserve to have a life that facilitates peace, happiness and growth. Embrace that wholeheartedly.

{87}

STOP ASKING "WHY DON'T THEY?" START ASKING "WHEN WILL I?"

Sometimes, I look at people with influence or power and wonder why they do some of the things that they do. Then, I remember something very important. I can't devote time to judging the actions of others without holding that same magnifying glass up to my own life. Most of us aren't celebrities or part of the global elite, but we have domain over our own actions. It's infinitely more rewarding and empowering to shape your own life and help the people around you than it is to wait for someone else to see things from your point of view.

{88}

GOING THROUGH YOUR TRIALS MAKES YOU INTO THE PERSON YOU'RE MEANT TO BE.

What if Michael Jordan never got cut from his varsity high school basketball team? Would he have the chip on his shoulder that pushed him to become the greatest of all time? We might never know. What about you? Have you ever thought about what kind of person you'd be if your life never forced, pushed, or inspired you to get better? Problems require solutions. Overwhelming situations call you to rise to the occasion. Rest for a second, but after you take a break, remind yourself that the situations you endure make you into the legend you're meant to be.

{89}

YOU CAN CONQUER ANY AND EVERYTHING THAT LIFE THROWS AT YOU.

Some days are easy. Some days you get punched in the face. These punches could be literal or metaphoric, depending on what kind of life you're living, but that's not what's important. What's important is that you continuously push yourself to keep moving forward, no matter how difficult a situation may be. You're so much more powerful than you give yourself credit for. You can endure more than you think. Situations might feel overwhelming in the moment, but allow yourself the time to recover and continue on with your mission. Your goals are so much more important than your obstacles.

{90}

NEVER APOLOGIZE FOR PUTTING YOURSELF IN A POSITION TO GLO.

Life is fluid. People are coming and going; situations are changing, and life is just doing its thing. A lot of the change in your life is out of your control, but you can't neglect the degree of agency that you do have. Persistently hold on to things that help you grow. Persistently push away the things that hold you back. Some things that limit you could help someone else. We're all different. Don't put the burden of being the perfect fit for someone else onto your shoulders when it might not even be a burden that's meant for you.

{91}

TAKE CHARGE OF YOUR LIFE, NO MATTER WHAT IT TAKES.

If you're not in control of your life, then who is? Another person. Another imperfect, self-prioritizing, mortal human being who is no better than you are inside. It's no secret that the world is unfair in countless ways. A baby born into elite wealth is no better than a baby born into extreme poverty, but the former is likely to have exponentially more opportunities than the latter. If you're not in the position you want to be, rebel decisively against the constraints limiting your ascent until they give way. Your situation might not be fair, but it's yours. Embrace it.

{92}

CLUTCH PLAYS MAKE THE HIGHLIGHT REELS, BUT CONSISTENT EXCELLENCE BREEDS CHAMPIONS.

I love watching NBA stars make clutch shots - improbable shots dropping through the net as the shot clock hits zero. The ensuing adrenaline rush. Few things on earth can compare, if I'm in the audience. You know what's better for the team that's playing? Undeniable victory. Beating the opponent every possession of the game. It makes life easier. Don't shy away from stepping up to the plate and delivering when the pressure is on, but don't let lack of pressure serve as a sign that you can stop moving the needle. Push the envelope consistently. Don't leave results to chance.

{93}

IT MIGHT TAKE LONGER THAN YOU EXPECT, BUT YOU'LL STILL MAKE IT HAPPEN.

If life happened the way I expected it to when I was 13 years old, I'd already be a wildly successful millionaire with a happy family, along with a taste for cigars and fine wine. In real life? Well, I have a taste for cigars and fine wine. Thanks, Dad. Believe it or not, life turned out to be way more complicated than adolescent me could have imagined. I'm sure the next year will have more challenges than I can conceive in the present moment. Regardless of what obstacles may come, I'll still find a way to live those dreams.

{94}

IF YOU HAVE AN AMAZING IDEA, BRING IT TO LIFE BEFORE SOMEONE ELSE DOES.

You have a great idea? Fantastic. Is it something nobody's put into action yet? Even better. Given the billions of people on Earth, how long do you believe your idea will remain within your imagination? If you wait to actualize your vision, how long until someone else does? Ain't no telling. A key component of a groundbreaking idea is its ability to solve a problem affecting many people. You better believe that if a problem affects many people, brilliant minds are searching for solutions. Choose to bring your greatest ideas to life today, or someone else will execute them tomorrow.

{95}

FIND YOUR NICHE. MASTER IT. WIN.

Don't create a plan with goals that are vague enough for you to get lost in. Don't set out to accomplish what's already been done. Don't allow a vague daydream to pass for a well articulated vision. The more specific your mission, the more efficiently and purposefully you're able to execute it. Taking the time to envision a final destination that's unique enough to merit the fulfillment of your unique potential is easily worth the effort required. You only have but so much time on this Earth. Finding specific reasons to maximize that time makes every single day more fulfilling.

{96}

PREPARE YOURSELF TO WIN BEFORE THE PRESSURE BUILDS UP.

Becoming an amazing free throw shooter doesn't happen when you step up to the free throw line in the last minute of the fourth quarter with the game on the line. It happens weeks, months, and years in advance when you're working on your form, focus and follow through in practice. You have to build a mental and physical foundation so strong that when the pressure is on, shooting is purely instinctive. You've already repeated the process thousands of times, to the point that you don't even have to think about the shot. You just take it, and you win.

{97}

DON'T WAIT FOR RECOGNITION. KEEP DOING THE WORK, AND IT'LL COME.

Energy can spark transformative change when consistently channeled into the right places. It's also extremely finite, like the general public's tolerance for Miley Cyrus. You gotta invest your energy into the right outlets. It's easy to waste energy seeking outside validation. Validation is invaluable to your success, but only acknowledging and appreciating specific types of external validation is limiting and harmful to your spirit. It can lead to pessimism, indifference and inaction. Allow yourself to appreciate the support that comes, but don't channel your energy into seeking specific types of validation when you could be focusing on the work instead.

{98}

THERE'S NO OPPORTUNITY WORTH DIMMING YOUR LIGHT FOR.

You're blessed. You're brilliant. You're exceptional. The question is, will you actualize the greatness you've been divinely equipped with, or will you allow it to lay dormant indefinitely? Many people choose the latter. We all have to sacrifice personal progression, at times. Life is complex, and a good portion of what happens is outside of our control. That being said, a situation that requires you to permanently remain beneath your potential is not deserving of your long term energy or effort. Understand that no one will tell you when it's time to pursue greatness wholeheartedly. It's entirely up to you.

{99}

NOBODY'S ICONIC UNTIL THEY EMBRACE THEIR IMPERFECTIONS.

Greatness isn't iconic by itself. People who accomplish incredible things become iconic and unforgettable when we can see little pieces of ourselves within their stories. It's empowering to see people with flaws as visible as our own maximize their potential. We respect people who change the world, but we don't personally embrace them as heroes unless we can identify with the weaknesses they've overcome and the imperfections that they openly embrace. You're never going to be perfect. Choosing to embrace your flaws and turn them into inspirational points for other people is a revolutionary act. Allow yourself to be imperfect.

{100}

YOU NEVER BECOME A LEGEND UNTIL AFTER THEY HEAR YOUR STORY.

It's easy to get caught up in the moment. It's easy to simply react when things don't go as planned, but remember that the way you overcome today's obstacles is important - to you, and to others who can be inspired by your story. You can never predict how people will receive your story until after it unfolds, but you can choose to push forward despite whatever plot twists may come. Obstacles might seem insurmountable. Situations could feel unfair. You might be tested in ways that you never anticipated. Choose to rise to the occasion. Your story is far from over.

CONCLUSION

I've endured some painfully dark moments during my time on this Earth, many of which were my fault. I've felt almost completely alone. I will never forget those moments of darkness, no matter how many times I try to erase them from my memory or pretend that they don't affect me anymore. I've healed, but I'm not the same. Those low moments shaped me.

Miraculously, those moments pushed me to fall deeper in love with my writing as a form of self-therapy. The moments that I didn't have the strength to speak of out loud spilled out onto pages, journals, and Google Docs. I threw in plenty of humor and sarcasm as a reminder to myself that I should still find a reason to smile. This book wouldn't exist if not for my darkest moments.

I'm never going to pretend like I'm happy every day. I'm never going to pretend that my life is perfect or my fate is guaranteed. I've contemplated throwing everything away. I've contemplated driving far, far away with the hopes that no one would ever find me or think about me ever again. Fortunately, I've learned to find the silver lining in my struggle. Have you?

ABOUT THE AUTHOR

Michell C. Clark is a social influencer and cultural curator from Woodbridge, Virginia who honed his sharp, witty writing style on social media as a means to connect with like-minded people during his years spent at a military academy. He writes to process past traumas, roast himself, and help others experiencing similar struggles. Michell has been featured in Billboard, Rolling Out, and JET Magazine for his entrepreneurial accomplishments. He's a Virginia Commonwealth University alumnus and a member of Kappa Alpha Psi Fraternity, Inc. Michell publishes an article and playlist every single week via his #MakeEmailGreatAgain newsletter. You can sign up at michellcclark.com. Michell just put a hashtag in his author bio because he's one of those damn millennials.

CONNECT WITH MICHELL C. CLARK ON SOCIAL MEDIA

TWITTER.COM/MICHELLCCLARK

INSTAGRAM.COM/MICHELLCCLARK

FACEBOOK.COM/MICHELLCCLARK

YOUTUBE.COM/MICHELLCCLARK

LINKEDIN.COM/IN/MICHELLCCLARK/

JOIN HIS EMAIL LIST AT BIT.LY/GREATEMAIL

CPSIA information can be obtained
at www.ICGtesting.com
Printed in the USA
LVHW06s0051290918
591750LV00009B/40/P

9 780998 970257